Learning How to Fall

T0169992

Lynne Rees was born and brought up in south Wales, and moved to the Channel Islands in 1978 to work as a currency dealer for an offshore bank. She has lived in Florida and Barcelona, and in 1985 settled in Kent where she ran her own second-hand and antiquarian bookshop for twelve years. She holds an MA in Writing from the University of Glamorgan and is the recipient of a Hawthornden Fellowship. She now teaches creative writing for the University of Kent and was awarded the Faculty of Humanities Teaching Prize in 2004. Her first book-length work of fiction, *The Oven House*, is published by Bluechrome. Visit her website: www.lynnerees.co.uk

Learning How to Fall

Lynne Rees

PARTHIAN

Parthian
The Old Surgery
Napier Street
Cardigan
SA43 1ED

www.parthianbooks.co.uk

First published in 2005
© Lynne Rees 2005
All Rights Reserved

ISBN 1-902638-60-3
    9 781902 638607

Editor: Richard Gwyn
Cover design by Lucy Llewellyn
Printed and bound by Dinefwr Press, Llandybïe, Wales
Typeset by type@lloydrobson.com

Published with the financial support of the Welsh
Books Council.

British Library Cataloguing in Publication Data

A cataloguing record for this book is available from the
British Library

This book is sold subject to the condition that it shall
not by way of trade or otherwise be circulated without
the publisher's prior consent in any form of binding or
cover other than that in which it is published and
without a similar condition including the condition
being imposed on the subsequent purchaser

Acknowledgements

Acknowledgements are due to the editors of the following journals and anthologies in which some of these poems, or versions of them, appeared: *Agenda, Connections, Envoi, The Frogmore Papers, The Interpreter's House, Iron, Magma, New Welsh Review, The New Writer, The North, Orbis, Poetry Ealing, Poetry Wales, The Rialto, Seam, Smiths Knoll, Stand, Writing Women, Teaching A Chicken to Swim – New Writing From Glamorgan* (Seren, 2000), *Reactions 2* (UEA, 2001), *The Pterodactyl's Wing – Welsh World Poetry* (Parthian, 2003), *Litfest 26* (Litfest, 2003), *Four Caves of the Heart – An Anthology of 14 Women Poets* (Second Light Publications, 2004). *Float* was broadcast on the BBC World Service – *Poems by Past*.

Grateful thanks to South East Arts for a Writer's Bursary, and to The Hawthornden Trust for a month of nurturing and inspiration. And to the 'Spa Girls' – Susan Wicks, Mara Bergman, Caroline Price, Mary Gurr and Sarah Salway – love and thanks for all your insights and encouragement.

Contents

For Tony

To live more in the emotions is to fall. One must literally take on weight.
Marvin Bell

They were but my visits, but thou art my home.
Matthew Prior

At Two

We stiffen our bodies like old bones
when you plant us in buggies, high chairs,

or slip like fish from your grasp
in the retreating tides of baths. You feel

the thumps of our plump fists,
our nails ragging the tender flesh

beneath your eyes. We hide small objects
in our ears, noses, or let them lodge

in the corridors of our soft throats. We scream
when you pick us up, put us down, comb our hair,

try to measure our toes. We pinch cats, stretch
our hands into the drooling jaws of dogs.

We burn up in the early hours and practice
the art of projectile vomiting

to send you scuttling for the phone.
We hurl ourselves face first into water,

sidle through the gaps between cars and watch you
pale as we back away from you smiling.

The Time-Stealer

I dread his step outside, his raincoat
always belted, hands fisted into pockets, eyes
searching through glass for time on my wrists

and shelves, the sweep of hands on watches,
alarms, old clocks – white faces trapped
inside a case of wood. Or at the kerb,

a shoulder tilted to my empty car,
waiting for the minutes to grow, his head
dipping to the blink of numbers, a slow

deliberate check. He is insatiable for it.
He will have me give it all to him.
He will have my heartbeats if I let him.

Visitors

We know they are coming,
the note slipped under the door
warns us of the time, their desire
not to disturb. The footsteps begin

at eleven, their charted lines
of longitude and latitude leading them
to this pinhole on the map,
their hushed chatter as if
the last thing they want on earth
is to wake us.

By three they are pegging out the land,
small wooden stakes thumping into the ground
around our house. And before dawn
we creep downstairs to slide the bolts,
fasten the shutters, pull the curtains
tight. We even tape up the letterbox.

At first we can ignore them –
their laughter, the noisy way they eat,
the singing late into the night,
the occasional call for us
to come out and sit in the sun.
But by the end of the week

one of us will argue
we were hasty, from the start
there was nothing to be fearful of,
that we misread their intentions.
And one of us will sneak down
in the dark to unbolt the door.
One of us will be laughing
as the key turns in the lock.

One Day The Wind Began to Blow and Didn't Stop

But it was fun – we laughed
at the twisting columns of leaves,
our neighbour's patio set blustering down the street,
ourselves leaning into it, how it knocked
the breath back into our lungs. We held each other
in the shelter of trees, planned to outrun it
hand in hand across a field. It didn't last.

We grew to hate the whip of it, car doors snapping
from our grasp, lips chapped, scalps gritty
with dust. We stayed in, arranged our lives
on the Web – money, books, food, wine –
got used to the way the house constantly creaked,
gave up filling cracks in the bedroom walls
and time-tabled our days to check the garden pots,
anchor them with stones.

Sometimes, when the weather warms up
we take off our clothes in the garden
and watch them tugged from our hands,
circling upwards like ragged birds of prey.
It nags at the small places on our bodies –
the creases at the corners of our mouths,
the tight plains at the backs of our knees.

We dream of boats mirrored on lakes.
We end our prayers with words of calm.
We ache for rain to fall vertically.

When we glance outside
and see someone fighting the thrust of it,
we mutter *Fool*, though our necks prickle
and stretch for a last glimpse, a coat
billowing like a sail, or a mouth
sealed to something like a smile.

Turned

Vinegar whiff,
hangnail,
crush of a rusted Coke tin –

I have let meanness in.
My mouth sifts its cold ash.

Yesterday
a glitter of insects
outside my window, leaves
a flush of applause
I cannot hear

today.
Insects bicker.
Curse of a wasp.

How long this pick and scrape,
this blind against the world,
apple savouring its worm?

Ripe Fruit

While I am choosing beefsteak tomatoes in Good Earth,
I see her in the distance marching down Pacific Avenue,
bare breasts swinging. She is laughing. I look away,
concentrate on my hands – their own two pounds of ripe fruit.

She passes the split window of the grocery store. Her breasts
are huge, humungous icing bags of flesh slung from shoulders,
but brown from the sun. Her skirt is blue and long. Her open
shirt flares in the breeze rolling up Pacific from the sea.

There are police at the intersection. Will they stop her there?
Will she help them bundle her breasts back into the flimsy
                                                    cotton
of her shirt? Will she resist them, or quietly watch as they
                                                    fumble
with each one, embarrassed at the weight in their hands
threatening to break free from the rickety clutch of buttons?
Will she still be laughing or will she start to cry,
wondering why the morning had to come to this?

Fat

Skinny women order his fish
fried in low-cholesterol oil,
batter as crisp and sheer as glass.

He teases them about goose-fat,
the slip of it, how it dimples
under fingertips, at the right point
of tenderness how it gives
to the tip of a tongue.

He dreams of women
whose flesh parts for him
like lard – their overlap, the spill
and pleat of them, his hands skating
over their suety gleam, their excess
rejoicing under his palms.

Shower Scenes

I

A noise you think you hear
under the pulse of water then dismiss
then think you hear again. You turn off
the flow, finger the certainty of the tap
and hold your breath, your heart
a steady thump. There's a choice now –
a chair scraping on the wooden floor,
the suck of air from the fridge's rubber seals,
or a tapping that sounds like a coin striking
a table top. For some reason
this one worries you the most.

II

You try and move soundlessly
but everything is amplified – the shower curtain's rings
clang like bells, your feet thud on the bathroom rug,
even the towel rasps your shoulders
like sacking dragged across boards.
And there it is again –the tock of metal on wood,
someone measuring time.

III

You open the bathroom door and peer
into the unlit hall. The kitchen door's a cavernous gloom
miles away. If only you could hear us shouting
Stay where you are! or *Put the light on*!
you might make it through the night. But you won't,
of course. You'll pad nearer and nearer to the noise,
through the surge of invisible music.
You call out the name of someone
like a prayer. Your mouth is dry,
your skin cold. You're a dead woman already
only missing the rope, the knife, hands
around your throat, the stink of breath.

Late

My mother said *Girl*
you'll be late for your own funeral.
She was right
but who could blame me for wanting
a last look at the waves,
the smell of salt.

And you know the timelessness
of the sea and what was meant to be
a glimpse became three hours.

I picked up the sensible court shoes
and ran along the quay
through the town's busy streets
regretting the choice
of Friday afternoon, the flesh coloured tights
fraying on my feet
but what struck me most
was the effortlessness of that run –
the silence of my heart
not a single squeeze of lung.

As I cornered the crematorium gates
and saw them hunched together
in the porch I thought of running
straight past their stricken faces
and across the memorial lawns
as if this was what I was made for

as if this was how I'd always
planned to spend the day.

White

She tackled the flat first, painted walls and ceilings,
re-tiled the bathroom, laid a carpet – a thick
marshmallow pile that crept between her toes
and fingers. That prompted her
to remove the mauve from all her nails.
White would be her god from now.
She'd been through Designer Clothes,
Foreign Foods – she'd delivered monologues
on sushi – and then New Age.
Well, she had her own idea. An Original.
She'd be the one they talked about
in years to come. The one who started White.
She fitted high watt bulbs in every room,
bleached her hair and eyebrows platinum,
a double pack for maximum strength
and removed all other body hair.
But still she thought how positively dark
she looked in all this light, how much her hips
resembled pork against the marble bath.
She tried bathing according to the books
on purification, adding a capful of bleach
then five more, but the skin around her nails
began to peel. And even though
she'd drape herself in white from head to toe,
the colour of her hands and neck would interfere.
She began to hate the evening, the way
shadows insinuated through her room
and how the morning burst upon her
with its blue. She kept the halogen on
night and day and the curtains drawn.

White rice, white sugar, white bread. She loved
the translucency of reduced fat, skimmed milk
or Pernod poured on ice.
Since the bleach hadn't worked she took
to dusting baby powder on her face and lashes,
painting her lips with skiers' balm.
She dreamed of snow
ran her hands along the ice walls
of her freezer, turning it to number six
so she could watch them grow, the meeting
of her breath with ice breath as she opened the lid.
She tried sitting in it and suddenly understood –
it wasn't her skin to blame. It was her blood.
She checked out all the clinics, got the best.
I want white blood she said at the desk.
The nurse just smiled, said *Sign here*
and *How will you be paying*?
How right she felt watching her blood
pump away to surplus stocks while she filled
with a master blend of glucose and salt.
Why hadn't she thought of this before?
After all, her bones were white. She knew
from the time she'd snapped her wrist,
the break so clean, so sharp, she'd seen
the ivory shear through her skin.
All those years of mistakes and fashion fads.
But this was The Look she was after.
She could see the magazine reports,
the glossy pictures – white leather,
alabaster walls, limed wood,

the bloodless silk of sheets absorbing
her barely perceptible frame.

She Forgets What She Wants

She can be hurrying to the Post Office
or ironing last week's clothes
or reaching for a carton of milk in a supermarket aisle

when she has to stand quite still. And still
she can't make out what it is
but it feels full of air and possibly pale yellow
or a blue more like a grey, and if it was a shape
round like a beach ball she had as a kid –

so light it seems to defy gravity, take an age
to complete its arc through the air
to where she's waiting, the thump of need
in her chest, hands trembling against the sky.

Teaching A Chicken To Swim

Each Sunday she unwrapped a pimpled bird
from its cardboard tray and cling film,
cut away the string to free the headless body –
loosening wings and plump, bound hips –
and gently laid it in the bath. Sometimes
the water filled the yawning hole
or leaked between flesh and skin
and bubbled into blisters. She persevered,
couching the bird in open hands,
urging it to try, to slice the water
with its featherless, aerodynamic wings.
She needed the inert frame to pull away,
splaying those irregular fins
and march its cropped and wanting legs
along the length of bath, turning at each end
as neatly as a chicken on a spit. She needed
just one successful launch.

Spontaneous

It happened at the Turkey Farm.
Witnesses heard a *woomph* like someone
stepping smartly on a bag of air and when
they got there, found the charred remains
of cloth, some bones. And a man
in Minnesota had done it on his deck at home,
mid-morning, the temperature only 54
but the Budweiser in his glass was warm.

If she could do at will what all these people
did in error, she reckoned on a money-spinner,
all sorts of side-lines – self-help books like
How to Find the Warmth Within. She'd start
small, spend days imagining the glow
of an orange ball inside her chest. Then weeks
focusing on the hairs along her arm until
she could feel and smell the heat, hear

a crack like a mosquito on an outside light.
She knew she was on a roll. Soon she'd be
hiring halls to accommodate the crowds.
She'd open with a nest of leaves transformed
to a smouldering pyre on her palm,
and build to her grand finale – the full
combust, walls racketing with applause,
the diminishing calls of *Encore*!

Horizons

For Nicholas van der Vliet

You don't know why
but after you set the question –
'*Discuss and Analyse the Use of Discourse and Field Specific Lexis
in Richard Dawkins'* The Blind Watchmaker *Chapter One*' –
you turn and gaze out of the window
and notice how the horizon curves like a bow
and wonder if a boy on a toboggan
could slide down it.

Your breath mists the window.
You draw a smiley face and underneath,
the words 'yeah, wicked' or even 'get a life'.
You hear the low rumble of voices behind you
but there's no going back now –
        you throw
your jacket on the floor, slip the knot of your tie,
flick your elbows into the Funky Chicken
and strut across the front of the Activboard.

One of the girls suggests you might like to
sit down, another is running for the Head
but someone at the back of the room is clapping.

Harlot Reveals All

...and I saw a woman sit upon a... beast... having seven heads and ten horns. And the woman was arrayed in purple and scarlet colour, and decked with gold and precious stones and pearls, having a golden cup in her hand full of abominations and filthiness of her fornication.

The Book of Revelation 17:3&4

Fridays were his nights.
He didn't rough me up like some other johns,
bought me presents, paid up front.
So I didn't mind the games, all that silly stuff
of draping me in scarlet cloth, not a stitch beneath
except the cheap paste he insisted that I wore.
Then he liked to ride me, call me his wild beast
until he fell exhausted into my arms, whispering
Baby, *Baby* long into the dark.

One night the neighbours saw him leave.
He never came again.

When I read all those things he said about me,
I had to laugh. *Filth and fornication* – so old fashioned!
I see him now and then on TV, the Born Again Prophet,
his hair still the colour of whisky.

Me? Well, business did slack off a while
(publicity doesn't always pay in my line)
but now they're back and more.
All that talk of heads and horns
must have done the trick.

Playing God in the Shallows

Around your bare feet, suddenly, a small city –
weed-covered pebbles like green parks
studded between neighbourhoods;
the spill of stones – blue and red roofs, white
blurs of drives; watery streets curling
round churches, furniture stores, even
a car-lot's glittering hoods and trunks;
and the sand sucked away here –
quarries, ravines. You could almost pick out

the Watson place – an old Chevy on blocks
in the front yard. But if you lean closer,
squint, the roads aren't roads at all
but a river in flood, the lowlands swallowed,
roofs anxious smears in the cloudy surge.
And more rain to come. Just think –
you could lift a foot and end it all, wipe out
the wails of children clinging to the pitch,
men and women fighting the lash of water.

Instead you stand back and listen
to a party on Boydell, the tinny music
and laughter, the hiss of ring-pulls,
someone nudged into the pool. Each day
brings what it brings or at least that's what you say
when you get up each morning – a small god
patting the heads of your bright-skinned kids –
and head off to work, cursing traffic
at the intersection, sure of where you're going.

Flood

While we sleep we create a flood – the hose
forgotten in the pond until our yard is a lake
feeding a river that creeps towards

our neighbour's house, coursing through
their dreams. Soon they are calculating wood
they'll need from resinous trees, the length

in cubits, the names of every living creature,
two of each. Hooves echo on un-planed floors.
And us like lofty gods in our attic room,

safe from the water building to a torrent,
picking up their compost heap and rockery,
a miniature wheelbarrow, its tortured tree

and sweeping them towards the Downs.
But we wake in time, paddle out through the dark
to stem our unholy flood. And they will see

the tide-marks on the drive, fingers of damp
reaching for their door, the cracks
of paving stones with traces of our intent.

The Woman in the Gutter

The woman in the gutter dressed very nicely
for someone in her position.

She didn't seem to mind if people
stopped and stared, or stepped over her.

Passing cars blew up leaves
and she brushed them away.

She even had patience with chewing gum.
A dog shat on her once and she

reapplied her lipstick, waited
three days for it to rain.

Once, when I was waiting to cross
I felt a finger brush the curve of my heel.

But I may have been wrong.

The Ladies' Annual Pocket Book

For the Year of Our Lord 1769

Could he have known she yearned for silks,
a fan of ivory and lace, a choke of pearls,
silver buckles, a new chinchilla muff?
Instead, he bought a Pocket Book;

100 and 4 pages for her cash accounts,
silk purse folds for the occasional coin
and printed at the rear, an essay
on the most deceitful vice of Luxury.

She never wrote a word or made a figure
count in all its pages; her memorandums
and appointments blank of dates and times.
Did she tuck it in a drawer or lose it,

accidentally, when walking in the early year,
dreaming of a tickle of pearls or that quizzing fan
from Gamble's in St. Martin's Court,
with peep-holes screened in silvered gauze?

But a wife maintained a modest pose.
She never even wrote her name.

Letting The Side Down

I am making a map of my left hand –
drawing a line past my wrist, around
the starburst of thumb and fingers.
I circle in nails, mark the flex of tendons,
folds of knuckles, each freckle and vein.

I want to have something to remember it by –
this useless hand that cannot write, or eat
alone, or catch a ball, this hand that shrinks
from meeting people, that sometimes hides
beneath tables and curls to a limp fist.

It is less than my left foot, my left eye;
at least they have a go at competing
with the right; this hand doesn't even try,
it trembles with the grip of scissors,
fumbles at doors, a full cup.

Stupid hand – I'll be better off without it.
Look how confidently the right grips
a knife, not a tremor, not even when
steel breaks skin; how unselfishly
it wraps itself around the stump.

The Crazies

We used to think they were foxes haunting the night.
Now we know better –

how they rise in the middle of storms, excited
by the thunder and crack, close in

easy as flood water over open land,
their wails raising the hairs on our arms.

And we know how to protect ourselves,
how we should close the windows, bolt doors,

how we should breathe slowly,
block our ears against their pleading,

our mouths from shouting back and urging them on.
But one of us always lets them in.

The morning after
we talk lightly about milk, road-works,

look past each other, eyes
raw with the night's unrest. It'll be days

before we dare to check the horizon, forget
who opened the door.

II

Amateur

Simple stuff at first – sad face/
happy face – my hand like a shutter

switching off the light in my eyes
then pulling joy back up from my chin.

Then 'pick a card, any card'
and mind-reading. I learnt

to palm coins, trinkets, silly
bits of glitter disappearing/

appearing from the nape of my neck
between my breasts. It was only

a small step to cutting myself
in half – I could juggle

balls, swords, fire
and be dancing at the other end of the room.

I practised holding my breath.
The Perspex tank was airtight, watertight,

padlocked on the outside.
But where do you go from there?

You're only as good
as your last trick, the rush of applause,

the sparkle of your name
on someone else's tongue.

I made myself disappear.

Like Water

A tendon flickers in your wrist like an eel
then flits between the channel of bones,
the pulse at the side of your neck
checks your heart's tide of blood, breath
ripples in your sleeping throat, and this reminds me
how sometimes you are like a great wave
rushing me along the coast of your life,
and other times like the shadowed corner of a pool,
the weight of water unfathomable

but most of the time you are like one of those trick taps
suspended over a pond, seemingly unattached
to any supply, but the stream of water
constant, clear, flowing up as well as down,
and me wanting to believe in the magic,
that you can defy gravity, that not all tricks
are in the eye, the sleight of a hand.

Snakes

Something big's dug a hole
in the lake's muddy bank, a whiskery snout
lurks in the shallows. I race home
through the forest to find you
drag you back across the swampy shore
past snakes you want to track
along fallen trunks
through weed and stinking water
where one whips out too fast
for you to pick up a branch.

Fear slices me awake –
a split tongue flickers
inches from my face. You're slipping
away – I can't remember the pattern
or the colours on the snake's back
and I wish you safe from snakes.
I wish I'd never gone down to the lake
on my own. I wish I knew
who should be saving who.

Who

A black and white woman cups her breasts
on the opposite wall, a fat lady perches
on the corner of your bath, her china mouth
a pinhole of surprise. Who are you?
I shift my thighs on the heat you left
on the toilet seat. I can smell you – piss,
your after-shave on two green towels.
Your toothbrush is damp in a glass.
No robe or comb. And who am I
creaking open a drawer and fingering
dental floss, a hotel shower cap,
nail clippers, a face I don't know
in the mirror specked with shaving soap
I wipe my finger through to join the dots?

No Man's Land

After we argue about 'Feminism' we don't touch
as if the bed has sprung up its own hostile curl
of barbed wire down the middle, sandbagged
dugouts with gun slots for the aim of a dark barrel,
the red eye of a cigarette to harden the mind.

We toss and turn all night, wondering if we'll ever
be safe, how our life seems to hang in the balance.
But this morning you risk sniper fire, the snare
of barbs, and nothing seems impossible
with your hand reaching across the cold.

The Snow Queen

Tough women always get bad press.
Cold. Bossy. Bitch. They said
I took him from the arms of his family
when he tagged along after me.

Ill-matched from the start
but I couldn't resist those young hands
on my skin. And though I've always been one for the cold,
a bracing walk, a bitter wind to blow a mood away,
I changed, spent days and nights sweating with him.

The week I went back to work,
I'd come home to find him buried under blankets,
the heating full on, his face as red as chestnuts,
not a scrap of housework done. Windows steamed
from his heat, his breath, his feet.
I slept in my own spare room

when I couldn't stand his body's furnace another night
while he spread hot and moist across my cool, white sheets.
The stench in the morning made me gag,
throw the windows open to his moans,
the condensation, the flowering of mould.
So don't tell me the old seduce the young.
He took me all the way.

The day I found him gone, I wept for joy,
for the cool setting on the shower,
the welcoming cold of the lavatory seat,
and then for fear of being alone. The bleak
expanse of mattress when I woke, a silence
that could decorate the walls.

It's months and I still miss the things
I grew to hate. Warm hands around my face.
At night, his heat rising against my spine.

Aphrodite

I liked to watch his arms, the way the muscles flexed
as he worked. I could make rivers run from the sweat
beading on his skin, by smoothing my hand
from the curve of his neck to those firm hills.
He was no looker but that body made me weep;
his thighs were as tight as iron.

The accident put an end to all that.
I watched him learn to walk again,
bent over at the waist, struggling
with the leg supports. If I tried to help him
he threw me angry words.

What else was I to do?
It's in my nature to be loved.

He found out, told all his friends.
Of course, they sided with the cripple.
I could hardly walk down the street
for winks and nudges, his mates balling their fists
and calling my name. I went away to the sea
to let things settle. He missed me so.

I'm more careful now. Sometimes
I watch him when he doesn't know
and those arms still make me feel weak;
they could crush a child as easy as eggs.

Stones at Cove Harbour

It possessed them until
they couldn't resist

surrendering
to ripples and folds –

here a woman,
hips tilting through shale,

legs taut,
belly an eclipse, there

a reef of muscle,
the swell

of a big man's thigh –
stone flesh

pulsing and softening
under the sea's rise and drift.

How limpets cling at low-tide –
this fierce our need.

Slugs

Let me come to you in wetness
sweet-sucking your mouth
slide around you
consume your most succulent trim.

Under moonlight
let us slither barely through short grass
shifting our weight as muscles contract
leave trails of silvery spittle.

Let daylight find us
locked together in some dark place
the weight of night still on our lids
our tongues moist with morning.

Fore-edge Painting

Wedding Gift for EM-DM London 1824

They must have wanted to know it, this secret
held between boards of red morocco
dressed in gilt, would have explored
beyond the covers, the lettering on the spine,
the binder's tooled dentelles, a flourish of gold.

They felt the leather in their hands, the raised bands
pressed against their palms, moisture passing
from skin to skin. Letting the front board fall
they arched the quire of pages to the left,
spreading the fore-edge against a thumb. Then

they uncovered each sliver of paper
disclosing its part – a crenellated tower,
a tree, the stone of a distant town,
and a road crossing water and hills, vanishing
into the indefinite colour of sky.

In The Middle

It seems to her they started in the middle,
not even a proper hello, they dived right in,
speaking to and over each other, no phone-calls
or dates for dinner before they went to bed,
kept discovering things they had in common –
a love of oaked chardonnay, buffalo mozzarella,

long dry kisses, staring, how they were both
caught masturbating at the age of five. Or
she'd call him from the store as she was reaching
for a pack of beer only to hear he was in a bar
lifting the same one to his lips. She imagined
living in the middle with him for the rest of her life –

watching him getting in, or out, of his car, picking up
on unfinished conversations, sitting down to meals
that somehow neither of them had cooked, his hands
finding the same places in her, again and again.
Though there had been one end: he walked out
on a Sunday evening and she listened to the gears

of his car changing on the hill, lay awake
in the middle of the bed watching the dark.
But he came back the next day at eleven –
they drank red wine, ate steak and kidney pie,
caught up in the middle of things again
and stayed that way. How lucky they are –

like the bright green oak leaf she picked
this morning, sap-rich with summer;
not the copper ones she stepped over, mottled,
their edges starting to curl, though something
in her made her look, the way they glinted,
seemed to have so much more to tell.

Your Heart

took a chance once
went skinny-dipping on a hot day
was striking out towards the centre of the lake
when the sun glittering on the surface like silver flakes
made it think of broken glass
and it raced to the shore,
safe again.
                    Since then
the trips it takes are short,
measured – around the block, a park
it knows the limits of, a door-key
like a talisman pressed against its skin.

And sometimes it shudders
awake from a dream
where it's pumping along a street
towards a double-decker bus
easing away from the kerb
the pole glinting
just out of reach.

Dermatoglyphics

The bloom in my palm is a measure
of the weight and heat of you.

The flush on the inside of my thigh
is the time you whispered *Wait* –

the deep pressure of your thumb
testing me like ripe fruit.

I can trace the lift of your hands
under the tilt of my hips

and track the blaze
of coming that first time.

And now this crease and furrow
is sleep refusing to draw in

and carved in the hollow of my throat
the ache of your name.

Rain

Rain is the sky's way of forgetting.
Mist drags over your face. You can only see
the gaps between trees, can't make yourself small enough
to hide from yourself and the windows
keep letting in rain.
                              Write 'cunt'
in salt on the kitchen table, imagine him
slipping into the hills' slatey folds, the earth
closing over.
                    Rain for days.
The river rocked with stones, the bridge carved
with someone else's name. You walk the lanes
sit on gates and watch sheep
mist shrouding the peaks
                              the sky trying to forget.

Anonymous

The problem for me is that I really don't want to be written about.

And she agrees
keeps him shackled
at the back of her mind
so how does he manage
to sneak onto every page –
the tick of a watch
a river in flood
a spring bolt
on a gate someone opens
then shuts, even lunch
when she writes the table
and he is every dish
she's ever wanted and she is
every mouth waiting to be fed?

When I Am Invisible

I will visit you at night,
lean over you to feel
the trickle of your breath
as you tip towards sleep, watch
the veins scribbled on your lids,
the flicker of you entering a dream.
I will trail you through
the minutes of your life,
press my footsteps
into the places yours leave,
stand behind you
as you wait for trains
to be touched
by the same breeze.
When you drive
you might catch the scent of me
rising with the car's heat,
and maybe one time
you'll think you see me –
a wrinkle of light in plate glass –
and I'll hear your heart's excitable beat,
watch your face settle
as you walk away, head dipped
in what might be relief.

How We Cry

My mother cries hard tears, tight
and slicing her face like steel.

My sister's tears are packed away, her eyes
balloons filled with water, their glassy skins
aching with weight.

I saw my father cry once – perched on the edge
of the tweed covered sofa in the living-room,
his father's death dragging
his face to his knees.

                      These days when I cry
I think of rain, how the sky falls down and blankets the hills,
fattens rivers to a torrent of mud; and how
a heron can still rise through it – away from the bruised banks,
a grey raggedy flight upstream.

III

Flying Over Greenland

Along the shore
the waveless sea's disguised
under a filigree of ice
like frost etched against glass
but further in the snow is thick,
sometimes crowned with rocks, and soon
there's only a soft ripple of white that goes on and on.

I'm so alone, my eyes ache
with the honesty of the sun. I can't believe
it will ever end – this is how I'll spend the rest of my life
staring down at this whiteness.

Under the pulse of air
I watch a quiver of white against white,
shivering folds rising towards me, but ahead
the land jigsaws into snow and sea. The sky
urges me on – faster, harder.

Falling

She's learning how to fall
off chairs, down flights of stairs
tripping off kerbs
into gutters or tumbling over
first floor windowsills
onto roads, pavements
slithering through tarmac
hardcore, wet clay.
She drops off cliffs
through ivy, fern
glancing off rock
to the glint of the river's skin
clatter of stones, silt.
At night she slips
into dreams – the mouth of a well
a roof's pitch, plunges
from room to room. Now
she only has to master
the sky, fall up
into the spiky overlap of leaves
through three layers of birdsong
over the horseshoe ridge of trees:
leaf, wingless thing
wiped clean by air, the spaces
between bedsprings.

Building

No doors or windows yet, no walls,
only the stud frames, and winking gaps

in old boards laid down
to stop us falling through. Not yet

the stairs to the cellar we imagine
will hold our wine, a table, two chairs.

Still the rickety ladder, the rough
stone to graze our knuckle bones. Still

the capped darkness, the trickle of water,
under our feet splinters of brick

as we follow the wall around
the soon-to-be-room – skeleton

smelling of earth and old rain –
past a door we've decided to forget,

its edges masked by shuttering struts,
a door that opens on a room

that holds a box
we've promised we'll never open.

In The Grain

Squint and there's a bird's eye,
a fingerprint, half a butterfly wing –

leaks of sap, tight knots,
some popped, replaced with glue –

here a porcupine, a limp fish,
the dark sockets of a skull,

and this panel where the wood
is sliced against the grain

and all roads lead nowhere or back
on themselves. I retrace

my journeys over and over again.
Now – the pull of a black hole,

or a bleed of sunset, maybe
light swelling the sky.

The Path

What woke you last night –
screech of owls,
the moon smothered by clouds?
This morning a fracture
of tail-feathers on the path,
wind scouring the glen,
your own breath sucked in
through clenched teeth,
and this bush choked by holly –
green berries hard as stone.
Don't touch them. Don't stray
into the tangled woods
with your gift of fruit,
your feet twisting in hollows.
Don't look up
through the cracked
kaleidoscope of leaves
to see what that cawing is,
the world tipping, your heart
unsure where it belongs.
Go back.
　　　　At the place
you started from, an open door,
heat, a man and woman laughing –
voices you will begin to recognise.

Eve

She takes off her clothes, stands naked in the garden,
but she still doesn't feel quite right – 5:30 in the afternoon,
the sky weighing its thunder. Then the rain comes in
on a wind, thick fingers wrapping her shoulders,
pooling her feet on the path. She opens her mouth
and knows she will die of thirst if she has to stay here.
If only she could drop the clothes she's holding
and dance right through that gate, out of this garden.
If only the thunder could teach her how to move.
She sees a flick of curtain, feels eyes scaling her body.
Wet trails of hair slither on her back. She should go in.
When he comes to the door, sees her tasting the rain
and yells *What are you doing?* she smiles. The sky
cracks above them. They may have to move.

Thursday Morning

It's there when I come back to check the level –
a sparkling planet
under the cold water tap,
grown from the bubble bath hurriedly poured – all this

while I yanked the duvet off the bed, separated whites
from coloureds, folded towels:
no god or mythical days of work or commanding words.
And there's more

where I rushed my fingers up and down the length of bath
to spread the cold, a galaxy
of foam – bobbing spheres, crescents, clusters –
you might lie on your back to wonder at, except

I'm looking down from the edge
of a neighbouring universe with my chin in my hands,
watching each rainbow glint and prickle,
how each moment exposed to air is full

of both light and loss. But I have to get on –
there's a bath to take, the laundry to be done,
a whole bunch of living creatures
waiting.

Hula-hooping with Dead Rabbits

You don't really notice them
at first, the silky fur only
a faint tickle under your feet
but as the heat seeps from your soles
you smell them – a musky tinge
to the whoosh of air – then you feel
the first twitch, faint thumps
with each roll of your hips
the swing of the hoop
      and the next minute

            they're all up
off their flat backs and dancing
some of them spinning in circles
noses to the floor doing 'the grass-nibble'
others up on their hind legs
swaying with you, their front paws
keeping a kind of hand-jive beat
          and you think
what good little movers they are, how ready
to unstitch themselves and let go
into the moment

      and so unlike the deer
on the next floor, brittle, ignorant
of each other on opposite sides of the room
that a shift of a neck could be the start
of something, or even a reminder –
the smell of rain in a thicket of trees
how heat passes from skin to skin.

Taking It All

Woodlice tighten into ball bearings under the mat.
Fish skulk beneath lily leaves.
Last week a frog camouflaged in the flower bed's damp earth.

But I am more like this pigeon waddling across the cobbles,
hopping onto the pond's brick lip, pausing
to enjoy the sun – my back
to the cat flicking and tensing at the lawn's edge.

I forget to look behind me, and ahead as well, and sometimes
I'm a flap of feathers, a squawk that goes on
for days, my heart a jelly.

But other times when I lift into the air,
the streak of cat stopped in its tracks at the filter wall,
it's all worth it – that moment
taken, sun on water, and my arms like wings
waving the world, and all it's got, towards me.

Penes

Like exotic pets, they have their tender side,
respond to love applied in varying measures,
a firm hand, a stroke to coax them out,

But they don't hiss or squeal, don't require
unusual meals of shredded fruit, humidity,
can travel without the need for quarantine.

And they're volatile in early morning light,
have a tendency to ignore commands,
display their feral side and roam at night.

So keep them confined, release with care.
They flourish under brisk handling; are reduced
to a fraction of themselves by a cold snap.

Crazy Cat Mugs

When we finish arguing I make you tea
in the mug with the fat, cross-eyed cat.

I have the cat with the big grin
bounding through a night sky.
The tips of my claws gleam.

You just sit on your arse, legs stuck out
in front of you, going nowhere
with a stupid look on your face,

while I, knowing better than you,
have nearly caught up with my own tail.

Moving On

From where I lie I can pick you up in an inch
of space between my thumb and finger, and put you
down anywhere – out onto the sea to bob along
in your metal framed, candy striped boat. Or here
next to me, so I can taste the salt on you.

Or along the beach among the sea cucumbers,
shrinking to millimetres as you travel. You're light
as the wind as I whisk you over the sand, and unaware
of your own fantastic journey – your muscles, limbs,
puppets to the pressure of my fingertips.

I can crush you, press gently until my thumb
and finger meet, squeeze all the sea water
out of you, rub the skin together until you're
just the grains of yourself. But I don't.
I return you to the place you chose, at the edge

of the sea, your back bent over and glowing
in the sun, liberating shards of seashells
from between your toes. I ease my fingers away
and your hand lifts, runs through your hair
as if missing the weight of something from above.

Float

You come across them
sucking the wet sand
or tangled in weed,
laces and heels missing, yawning
gaps between uppers and soles
and you line them up – espadrille,
trainer, a child's red Wellington –
toes pointing out to sea,
watch them rise
on the incoming tide, your fleet
of little boats setting out
on a big adventure, imagine
some of them finding it – their lost twin
nudging the crest of a wave, or washed up
in a place they never dreamt of.
Though most of them won't –
they'll sink, be tossed back to shore.
But what a sight, this flotilla
of leather, plastic and rope
dipping and rising
on the swell and roll. And why
don't you take off one of your own
and hurl it over the breaking waves?

Facing South

They rise from the shore,
a litter of birds blowing left and right
and settle again as we walk by –
gulls, sandpipers, terns, all facing south,
some with heads bent against their wings,
others staring straight at the sun.

And it's the same when we return –
the outfielders' warning,
a cloak of feather and cry above our heads
and the airborne confusion over
so quick, it seems their past
is un-travelled, the future eclipsed.

what's happening

my clock is throwing its voice across the room
my laptop starts its heavy breathing
the desk-lamp is busy
bleaching a patch on the wall

while I do nothing – just lie here and watch
a candle flame stretch
and bounce off molecules of air
an insect lit by the evening sun jumping at the windowpane

this morning when I opened the sash
a single spider thread slung from the sill
propping up the weight of the wooden frame –
no wonder

I had to lie back down
listen to the sighs of my un-sipped inch of tea
bubbles in the water carafe gossiping at the glass
an apple on my dresser one long golden yawn

Riding the Donkey

Except it's not – it's a deer
cast in iron with antlers of horn
and bolted to the ground
but that's what he feels like
when I'm up on his back

clicking him into a trot
around the lawn, and these walls
are not so high and the sea
not that far away
we can't smell the salt.